POEMS,

EARLY AND LATE.

BY

HORATIO NELSON POWERS,

AUTHOR OF "THROUGH THE YEAR."

CHICAGO:

JANSEN, McCLURG & CO.

1876.

The Riverside Press, Cambridge.
PRINTED BY H. O. HOUGHTON AND COMPANY.

TO CLÉMENCE.

It has been your lot to suffer, and to be denied, withal, a good deal that is suited to soften the hardship of your secluded life. But trial has not repressed your sympathy with whatever is engaging and ennobling in human existence; and you have never failed to make home attractive by a spirit whose patience and sweetness have hallowed all the years of our companionship. In some way that may assure you of my appreciation and gratitude I wish to connect your beloved name with this little cluster of verse — the offspring of my heart; but I can think of no words that will mean so much to you, or be so acceptable, as the simple statement, that

TO MY WIFE

I Dedicate this Volume.

H. N. P.

CONTENTS.

AT HOME.

NATURE AND LIFE.

AT HOME.

AT HOME.

SAINTS.

THEIR faces touched with radiance pure
and tender,
Holy and sweet with soft and mystic
light,
The Saints of old look on us, through the splendor
Of crowns, and thrones, and beatific sight.

But how remote and taintless of the earthy,
With their rapt eyes and brows of peerless
calm!
Are they alone, of all the ransomed, worthy
Of Heaven's high roll and the victorious palm?

We yield them reverence, yea, we bless the ages
By their great deeds and sufferings sanctified:
Still other names, on God's resplendent pages,
By theirs are fit to be inscribed beside.

For saints are with us in the lowly places
Of toil, and tears, and poverty, and sin;
The sweetest souls, the most unsullied graces,
Ripen amid the rough world's dust and din.

They move in common ways, unpraised, unheeded,
Accepting work that nearest to them lies;
Zealous to serve where most their help is needed —
Unconscious angels in an earthly guise.

In hut, and wayside place, and attic dreary,
The tasks of love they patiently fulfill,
Nursing the weak, and comforting the weary —
Their meat and drink the Master's blessed will.

Braving the world's disdain, neglect, and dangers,
Naught matters if their duty well is done;
Living each day as pilgrims and as strangers,
They are content if God's applause is won.

Worn brow, sweet voice, and cheek of hectic pallor
Tell of their inner strife and conquered pain,
Of self subdued, and the immortal valor
That learns through crosses heights of peace to gain.

O holy ones, ye make our households dearer;
Ye consecrate our hearths, and nights of woe
Ye bring the unveiled world of glory nearer,
And Christ to doubting, troubled spirits show.

ARISS.

As if an Angel had passed by
And left the odor of the sky,
So seems it now from room to room,
Still hallowed by her heart's perfume;
Something is sacred, something dear,
That had not been without her here.
Something is better, though we grope
Aweary with our broken hope:
Something above an earthly trust;
We know it is not "dust to dust."
.Our loves were so inwove and blent,
So rich in trust and calm content,
It did not seem that love could draw
Her from us by its mystic law.
Yet somehow, in her look and tone,
We felt she was not all our own.
Something within her nature bore
The fragrance of the heavenly shore: —
The bud could only blossom where
God's perfect smile was light and air.
A sweetness in and round her dwelt
Untold by choicest words. We *felt*

The pensive grace, the tender tone,
Like south wind over roses blown ;
Her artless trust, affection's calm,
That folded all her life in balm ;
Her genial fancies, insights new,
Her ways all simple, guileless, true ;
The warm soft feeling of the sky
That trembled, melted in her eye ;
Her quiet joy, the household care
She took ere she was half aware.
All this we felt, and deeper feel
In grief that time has failed to heal.
Ah ! music only could express
Her nature's subtle loveliness.
  How many pictures did we make
Of years to come for her sweet sake.
We saw her beauty gather bloom,
And love for deeper love make room ;
Her spirit ripen, as it drew
From all things lovely light and dew,
And, breathing sweetness everywhere,
Her life reach upward like a prayer.
Alas ! for summers never born,
For purple eve and golden morn,
For hearts that ache, and eyes that swim
In sorrow till the world is dim.
In her fair face we shall not see
The tenderness which was to be ;
We shall not feel, through quiet days,
The blessing of her graceful ways ;

The seasons shall not nurse and teach,
With soft caress and golden speech,
Her tender thought, nor shall we view
In her love daily something new,
Nor see Christ making lustrous white
The life he fills with peace and light.
Ah, vain lament! It is not here
That being finds its perfect sphere;
Her life is more than we can guess,
Enwrapt in the Divine caress.
It must be better — and we know
That all we love shall lovelier grow;
Shall wait to welcome our embrace,
Beneath the smile of God's own face.

THE OLD CHIMNEY-PLACE.

A STACK of stones, a dingy wall,
  O'er which the brambles cling and creep,
A path on which no shadows fall,
  A door-step where long dock-leaves sleep,
A broken rafter in the grass,
  A sunken hearth-stone, stained and cold,
Naught left but these, fair home, alas!
  And the dear memories of old.

Around this hearth, this sacred place,
  All humble household virtues grew,—
The grandsire's lore, the maiden's grace,
  The matron's instincts deep and true.
Here first sweet words were lisped; here broke
  Life's morning dream, and yet more dear,
The love that life's best impulse woke,
  Grew warmer, gentler, year by year.

How cheerful, while the storm without
  Muffled the earth and iced the night,
The ruddy glow gushed laughing out
  On merry groups and faces bright;

How chimed the crackling, freakish flame
  With rosy mirth or thoughtful ease,
Or, may be, syllabled the name
  Of one rocked o'er the shivering seas.

What fairy scenes, what golden lands,
  What pageants of romantic pride,
In the weird deep of glowing brands,
  Saw the fair boy, the dreamy-eyed,
Till musing here, his spirit drew
  Strong inspiration, and his years,
By Beauty's subtle nurture, knew
  The paths of Nature's inner spheres.

Here, as the swooning embers sent
  A faint flush through the quiet gloom,
In the warm hush have lovers blent
  The fragrance of their heart's fresh bloom;
And, veiling in soft-drooping eyes
  Her tremulous joy, here blushed the bride:
Here, o'er pale forms in funeral guise,
  Farewells from broken hearts were sighed.

This spot the pilgrim, 'neath strange skies,
  Saw in his wayside dream; here stood
Old friends with gladness in their eyes;
  Here grew the beautiful and good —
Sweet friendships — faith serene and sure —
  Manhood's strong purpose, warm and bold —

Courage to labor and endure,
  And household feelings never cold.

Here, leaning in the twilight dim,
  All round me seems a haunted air;
I hear the old familiar hymn,
  My heart goes upwards in the prayer
That made the night so full of peace;
  Kind lips are on my brow — my ear
Hums with sweet sounds — they faint — they cease —
  And night o'er all broods calm and clear.

A HYMN OF THE MOTHERS OF THE PATRIOT SOLDIERS.

HOME calls each loved, familiar name
  With precious mem'ries stored;
Deal gently, Lord! 'T was not for fame
  Our children took the sword.

We never thought when each young face
  First softly touched our own,
And little hands, with sweet embrace,
  About our necks were thrown,

That our own veins were nursing then
  The holy cause of Right,
And that from our own bosoms men
  Would spring to Freedom's fight.

We cannot deem the off'ring vain,
  Our dearest though we give;
Nor do we ask release from pain,
  If but the Nation live.

Still, sometimes, as alone we kneel
  Where once the cradle stood —

So much comes back — 't is hard to feel
  That all our grief is good.

The rosy cheeks so round and fair,
  The patt'ring little feet,
The laughing eyes and silken hair
  Of those whose touch was sweet,

Rise up amid the glare and din
  Of battles' fiery tide,
And flit past prison bars, within
  Which love is crucified!

We know we bade them go, when stirred
  The land from sea to sea,
For 't was Thy voice, O Christ, they heard
  Proclaiming liberty.

But oh, this travail long and sore,
  Seeing their thorny way,
And never able to do more
  Than serve at home and pray.

It seems as if the mother's hand
  Could soothe the suff'ring best,
And that the mother ought to stand
  By children laid at rest.

Forgive us all our doubts and fears
  While Thy great work goes on;

We do rejoice amid our tears,
  And pray, "Thy will be done."

Thy will — good will — its message now
  Of promised peace grows strong,
And, flashing on War's awful brow,
  Declares the doom of Wrong.

It is enough. Out from the gloom
  Rises a nation free.
Still, at the cross and by the tomb,
  We cling, O Lord, to Thee.

January, 1865.

THE ANGELS' BRIDGE.

WHENE'ER a rainbow slept along the sky,
The thoughtful child expected Angel bands
Would glide upon its gorgeous path of light,
With half furled wings and meekly folded hands:

For he had dreamed the rainbow was a bridge,
On which came bright ones from the far-off shore, —
A strange and pleasant dream — but he *believed*—
And his young heart with love's sweet faith ran o'er.

How full of dreamy hopefulness his face,
How many tender welcomes filled his eyes,
When for celestial visitants he watched,
In mute and holy converse with the skies!

The gentle child grew very wan and weak;
And as he lay upon the bed of pain,
One day of storm, he only meekly said,
"When will the 'Angels' Bridge' reach down again?"

In musing trance while gazing on the clouds,
A flood of sunlight lit the humid air,
And springing forth, as if from God's own arms,
A lustrous rainbow shone divinely there.

A tender smile played o'er the child's pale lips—
"Down the bright arch the white-robed Angels come,
Oh, see their shining pinions!—their sweet eyes!"
He said—and, 'mid their soft embraces, floated home.

OUR BOY.

He came, we know not how, 'mid fears,
And sorrows ripening with the years;
Dropped out of Heaven, in our distress,
Incarnate dream of loveliness,
Flushing to rose our cloud-draped days,
And voicing all our grief with praise.
His trustful eyes God's grace beamed through;
The earth in his sweet smile was new;
His life set all discordant strains
To glad harmonious refrains,
Interpreted the deeper speech
Our hearts would fain each other teach,
Bade us Love's vaster world descry,
And spelled its tenderest mystery.

He greets us now, a dancing beam,
In which Hope's deathless pictures gleam;
A flower on which Christ's peace is sent;
A star of Love's pure firmament;
A breath of Eden's lost perfume,
That scents the house from room to room;
A wingéd joy that hovers where
The old ache was so hard to bear.

A Poem is he, music fine,
Pure gold of life, inspiring wine.
The honey of the fragrant hills
In him its subtlest balm distills ;
The birds, the brooks, the purple seas,
The dawn's and eve's sweet mysteries,
The bloom that from the kiss of May
Bathes all the vales with tinted spray,
Faint moonlight glimmer, and the rare
Keen nectar of the mountain air,
Are in his soulful charm ; and more —
The things that haunt us by the shore,
And in old woods, and as we lie
Tranced 'neath the calm, blue, throbbing sky,
And strive to clasp the inner soul
That makes and glorifies the whole !

O precious gift ! We 're rich, though poor !
Ah ! Lord of Love, we pine no more.
Thy life is ours, dear radiant boy —
Home's light and angel, food and joy !
Gazing with surcharged hearts on thee,
We think how vast God's heart must be !

A ROSEBUD.

It was merely the bud of a blood-red rose
  That I found 'tween the lids of my book to-day.
What of it? Nothing to you, I suppose —
  Sweet ashes a breath would scatter away.
Yet here I am holding the dead, faded thing,
  As the sun drops out of the August sky,
And dew-drunken blossoms their odors fling
On the twilight air — do you ask me why?

The years are gathered in this little tomb, —
  (Strange that a grave in my hand I should
      hold,) —
Springs that showered their kisses of bloom,
  And summers that reveled in fruits of gold.
No breath of the meadows nor orange bough
  Sheds to my spirit an odor so rare.
You see not — how can you? — what I see now —
That marvelous face — are the angels so fair?

She gave me this bud and a single leaf, —
  Geranium — it has crumbled away; —
What a glory touched life then, but how grief
  Drives to tasks that sprinkle the head with gray!

Half doubting I number the seasons since flown;
  Like a star she just trembled on womanhood's
      eave;
To what in the garden of God has she grown?
  Naught more fair than she was can my fancy
      conceive.

For the roses of morning, and music, and light,
  The motions of birds, and the freshness of June,
The glimmer of lilies, and childhood's delight,
  In her exquisite nature were blended in tune.
Its sweetness yet lingers like perfume that clings
  To the air when the splendor of blossoms has
      fled,
More tender than touch of invisible wings,
  The spell of her presence around me seems shed.

And now while this faded bud in my palm
  Grows dim in the darkness, and still is dear,
All over my sorrow is sprinkled a balm
  From the depths of a heavenly atmosphere.
A hand long vanished I seem to hold;
  The years their glory of dreams restore;
I see a face that can never grow old
  And life looks large on the other shore.

THE NEW YEAR.

A FLOWER unblown ; a Book unread ;
A Tree with fruit unharvested ;
A Path untrod ; a House whose rooms
Lack yet the heart's divine perfumes ;
A Landscape whose wide border lies
In silent shade 'neath silent skies ;
A wondrous Fountain yet unsealed ;
A Casket with its gifts concealed : —
This is the Year that for you waits,
Beyond To-morrow's mystic gates.

Oh may this Flower unfold to you
Visions of beauty sweet and new ;
This Book on golden pages trace
Your sacred joys and deeds of grace.
May all the fruit of this strange tree
Luscious and rosy-tinted be ;
This Path through fields of knowledge go ;
This House with love's content o'erflow ;
This Landscape glitter with the dew
Of blessed hopes and friendships true ;

This Fountain's living crystal cheer,
As fail the springs that once were dear;
This Casket with such gems be stored
As shine in lives that love the Lord.

OUR SISTER.

HER face was very fair to see,
So luminous with purity:—
It had no roses, but the hue
Of lilies lustrous with their dew—
Her very soul seemed shining through!

Her quiet nature seemed to be
Tuned to each season's harmony.
The holy sky bent near to her;
She saw a spirit in the stir
Of solemn words. The rills that beat
Their mosses with voluptuous feet,
Went dripping music through her thought.
Sweet impulse came to her unsought
From graceful things, and beauty took
A sacred meaning in her look.

In the great Master's steps went she
With patience and humility.
The casual gazer could not guess
Half of her veiled loveliness:
Yet ah! what precious things lay hid
Beneath her bosom's snowy lid:—

What tenderness and sympathy,
What beauty of sincerity,
What fancies chaste, and loves, that grew
In heaven's own stainless light and dew.

True woman was she day by day
In suffering, toil, and victory.
Her life made holy and serene
By faith, was hid with things unseen.
She knew what they alone can know,
Who live above, but dwell below.

BONNIE.

UNDER the crimson trees that sighed,
Under the sod whose flowers were sere,
We laid our fair young Bonnie aside,
'Mid the hectic glow of the dying year.

Little the change to most indeed, —
A sunbeam less to gladden the earth,
A frail blossom broken, that few would heed ;
How mean is the great world's measure of worth !

Filling our hearts with a calm content,
Tinting our future with hues of gold —
How faded the lustre her presence lent
To common things, when her lips grew cold !

Tenderest face that won us so,
Softest eyes where we used to see
Love on its heavenly journey go, —
As God's will is, it is best to be.

Best, we trust, though the cloud is dark ;
The smiter to her was more than dear ;

Her spirit rose to Him as the lark
   Rises and sings when the sky is clear.

All for the best, though it seems not so —
   Losing our treasures that we may save,
Little of all love is can we know,
   Till we leave our darling asleep in the grave.

THE APRIL SNOW.

Four Aprils only had she known,
  Four days the pansies blew ;
The Spring, though scarcely half out-blown,
  Such sweetness never knew.

Her joy was in these flowers, they wore
  For her their tenderest grace ;
Sweet fortunes seemed for both in store,
  To see them face to face.

A cold cloud muffled up the blue,
  A shadow crossed the stair,
A strange fear chilled us through and through,
  Ere we were half aware.

Without, the darkness seemed to flow
  With sorrows never said ;
Within, our hearts heaved to and fro
  About a little bed.

Morn shook its light, a golden shower,
  On snows o'er pansies blown ;
Faith saw the shroud about our Flower,
  To marv'lous beauty grown.

Soon, from the wasted snow, the bloom
Of flowers glowed more bright —
So thought we she would leave the tomb
A radiant child of light.

ONE YEAR.

A YEAR of sweets — a little year
  That vanished with our darling's breath.
So strange ! it doth not yet appear
  What is the blessing hid in death.

One little year, yet oh ! how long,
  With such a love as made our light :
Each day was a delicious song,
  Whose rapture lasted through the night.

There came with him the keener sense
  Of what the perfect life may be ;
And sad years had their recompense
  In what he gave unknowingly.

The household voices caught his glee,
  The tasks of home were changed to play ;
The freshness of his infancy
  On every pleasant prospect lay.

How restful the contented heart
  Held his rare sweetness to its core,
And turned from empty shows apart —
  Rich in his riches, more and more.

O shining brow and golden hair
  And eyes that looked beyond the blue!
Dear face, that grew from fair to fair,
  The same, yet always something new!

A sweeter dream whoever dreamed
  Than came with his soft lips to ours?
Blent with his life, our being seemed
  Drowned in the glowing soul of flowers.

All through the years his beauty shone;
  His path and ours appeared the same;
And every good we called our own
  Was linked with his beloved name.

O heart of God that pities all!
  O Love that gives and takes away!
Confused and faint, on Thee we fall,
  Yet know not how we ought to pray,

Save this, that in our doubt and fear
  We wait as loving children should.
We cannot see nor far nor near,
  But trust that somehow all is good.

MONTHS AFTER.

SHE was so quiet in her ways,
Beside us she so meekly grew,
That, mid the cares of busy days,
How sweet she was, we scarcely knew.

Not much she spoke, and yet we read
Her wishes in her wondering eyes ;
But sometimes curious things she said
That filled us with a strange surprise.

Often alone amid her play
She listened as if friends were near ;
Who knows how much the angels say
That only little children hear ?

Ah, gentle one ! whose fair bright face
With such a light of feeling shone,
What might have been thy riper grace
Hadst thou to woman's stature grown ?

Could we have kept thee till our end
How different all our life might be.
Spirit of childhood, oh descend,
And mould us more and more like thee.

The birds come back on joyous wing,
And build and carol as before ;
The blossoms in the meadows spring ;
With beauty earth is pictured o'er ;

But flowers and birds increase our pain ;
She should be here with happy May ;
The sweetest vernal songs complain,
And nature grieves, though all is gay.

'T is true our sorrow colors all ;
She came but as a transient guest,
Still it does seem that she must call
For our love sometimes 'mid the blest :

That though her life is bright and fair,
She longs at times to press her cheek,
And nestle to the bosom where
She used to cling too glad to speak.

We know not what may be the bliss
Of those who walk the upper sphere,
But oh ! how much we need, in this,
The touch of those whose love is dear.

NATURE AND LIFE.

NATURE AND LIFE.

WITH BRYANT AT HIS BIRTHPLACE.

PON the hills where first he saw the day,
Broad shouldered hills, with dusky glens between,
And solemn groves of immemorial trees,
Where fountains gush, and birds of plaintive note
Make the strange stillness seem a living soul,
Past meadow slopes, down arcades of green lanes,
And over fields but little trod of men,
Mid stunted herbs and beds of straggling briar,
We rambled oft and long. Now strayed our feet
To the wild margin of the mountain stream,
And where the cornice of the woods hung low,
And in the orchard's forest-walled recess;[1]

[1] Mr. Bryant has a pear orchard of thrifty growth, some two or three acres in extent, on the very summit of his Cummington estate, two thousand feet above the sea, which is shut in on every side by a wood of lofty maples and beeches.

And then they paused where we could look afar
On village spires and homesteads in the haze,
As on a picture in the land of dreams ;
Or o'er huge highland-bosses, past DEERHILL,
To GREYLOCK silent in the Summer sky.
At times we sauntered on the public way,
Free from the scrutiny of curious eyes ;
And sometimes on the rocks, his youthful seat
At noon between the Sunday services,
In hollows where 't was twilight all day long,
On sunny summits, and by shaded spring,
We stood and lingered ; he meanwhile
Greeting with kindly converse all the shows
Of wondrous nature, quoting aptly verse
Of richest flavor, giving voice again
To old traditions of the place, which shed
A tender light on his own tender years,
And with such anecdote as genius tells
To make the Truth more like her own true self,
Coining the gold of wisdom as he spake.
And then, perchance, slight bent, with folded arms,
Rapt in the scene that filled his inner eye,
He walked a king of undisputed realms,
Unconscious of his greatness and his sway.

'T was here in this old forest when a boy,
As on him fell the seer's sacred fire,
He hymned his THANATOPSIS. This wild field
Contains the unmarked GRAVES that wooed his muse

To tender descant o'er the aged pair
Who sleep together on the lone bleak hill.
Here glides the little RIVULET whose birth
Is in the thicket's borders, prattling still
As in the Poet's childhood, and as sweet
As when it taught him his pathetic song.
Before the entrance to this noble wood,
For which the grand "INSCRIPTION" was designed,
We mused as by some hoary sanctuary,
And entering mid its coolness and repose
Talked in low tones of what is most august
In all the marvel of our human life.
There under the great canopy of green
He stooped and plucked, with the same reverent hand
That three-score years and ten had plucked before,
The YELLOW VIOLET — not the blossom now,
(For t' was midsummer), but the pods of seed,
And gave me. As he bent like one in prayer,
And lifted tenderly the lowly leaves,
And with caressing fingers showed me how
The plant was fashioned in its moist, cool bed,
I wondered at the thoughts that in his heart
Must blossom now, as Memory looked back,
And at the pictures of his pilgrimage
That rose and glowed before him, touched with hues

Of all that made his life so beautiful,
Since in fair youth he learned the lesson breathed
By this meek floweret of the early spring.

So passed the days, where in his manhood's strength
Returning to his native hills, he led
His fair young daughter with delighted eye
To look upon the landscape that he loved,
And where the blue FRINGED GENTIAN not in vain
Pleaded for trust in Heaven, and where he drew
The dazzling stores that make his WINTER PIECE;
Where, too, in these late years his thrifty hand
Had planted groves of larch and birch, and set
Orchards of pear and apple, built for miles
A highway firm along the mountain side
For public use, and where, with generous aim,
In a sweet nook beside the river's curve,
He reared a solid structure proof to fire, —
A Library free to all the country round.

Sweet days, like Sabbaths minist'ring life!
Walks, leading ever to a holier place!
A clearer air is round me, and calm forms
Of the immortals look upon my face.

August, 1876.

A VOICE IN THE DESERT.

The West was gorgeous with the sunset splendor —
The gathered flowers of light's resplendent crown;
Bloom after bloom did paradise surrender,
As if the gardens of the blest came down.

The East was piled with clouds of storm and thunder —
Huge mountains seamed with bolts of hurtling fire —
Now swept by gales that tore their cliffs asunder,
And then in weird convulsions heaving higher.

O'er the sun's couch the roses still kept blowing,
And royal lilies, starred with purple eyes;
And banks of golden daffodils kept growing,
Soft ridge on ridge, along the glowing skies.

But down the gorges of the storm's sierras
The rain and hail in roaring cascades fell;
The lightning, playing like a dance of Furies,
Pictured the nameless scenery of hell.

On the vast plains where I beheld the vision —
  On one side beauty, on the other dread —
Between the Tempest and the Scene Elysian —
  An antelope unfrighted bowed its head.

Beside a stunted shrub, alone, unfriended,
  It waited 'midst the awful desert place,
As if at home and tenderly defended,
  Eve's radiance and the storm-glare on its face.

I saw the dying of the western splendor,
  I saw the darkness of the tempest fall,
And heard a mystic voice, in accents tender,
  Out of the brooding Terror to me call:

"O wanderer o'er Life's deserts and its mountains,
  In storm and sunshine, with uncertain feet,
Pining for joy of the immortal fountains,
  And clinging still to all of earth that's sweet;

"One heart is in the thunder and the roses,
  One hand the honey and the gall distills;
He who upon the INFINITE reposes
  His place in Heaven's grand order meetly fills.

"Whate'er his path, however sad its seeming,
  The glory or the darkness overhead,
Upon it Love's unchanging smile is beaming,
  And to the perfect GOOD his steps are led."

ESTES PARK, COLORADO.

THE mountains lift their clear brows to the sun,
The sun upon each high-throned monarch smiles;
A glory poured from cliff to stream is won
By this free friendship, whose delight beguiles
The musing eye along the forest aisles,
The Snowy Range, torn scarfs of golden mist,
And where Long's Peak frowns o'er the lesser piles,
By one sweet cloud in dying rapture kissed
In its ethereal realm of rose and amethyst.

I lie beneath a music-breathing pine —
The sturdy harper of this highland vale—
Whose leafy dream is whispered into mine,
And hear the West Wind's soft, confiding tale,
The mystic legends of the thunderous gale,
O'er frozen peaks, voices of flashing floods
Down sunlit passes and in moonlight pale,
The weird traditions of the haunted woods,
And dark untrodden depths of these grand solitudes.

The lawns curve up like ocean waves that swell
  Against their rocky barriers and cease ;
Quaint porphyry walls unfold in many a dell
  Where the fawn feeds and sports in wild release ;
  In the sweet air coo unseen doves of peace ;
Through flowery gorges streamlets bring the news
  Of winter storms that left their snowy fleece
On yon white ridge, whose morn and evening hues,
Like garlands hung on high, their tender bloom diffuse.

Where else drank one from such a peerless cup ?
  This royal goblet scooped by God's own hand
From solid mountains, grandly lifted up
  And made amid a continent to stand —
  A Fount of Beauty poured for all the land !
For ages here has ripened Nature's wine.
  Not one of all the old Olympian band
Sipped as with sweet nectar to the soul as mine ;
I drink, and life grows large with ecstacy divine.

Well didst thou seek, Dunraven, this retreat,
  Turning from England's softer charms aside ;
Here in wild chase thy pulse shall healthier beat
  And pleasant pass the restful summertide ;
  No cares of state nor critic's pen shall chide,

Nor social follies irk the serious hour.
'T is not from man and duty thou dost hide,
But to train life to more consummate flower
And gain from Nature's lore a more benignant power.

The rose upon Long's regal forehead dies,
And a great shadow, flung by dark-winged Night,
Falls on the vale. In more majestic guise
The mountains tower in still and awful might;
The soft dusk vibrates with a meteor's flight;
Balsamic odors all the air embalm;
The stars look down in tremulous delight;
Heaven breathes to Heaven its utterless deep calm,
And with o'erflowing praise the river chants its psalm.

"THE STONE CHURCH."[1]

OUR path has been beside a mountain stream,
Up through a weird and wonderous ravine,
'Neath fragrant canopies of ancient trees,
And 'tween green tasseled rocks, that, 'mong the ferns,
Sleep like old Titans.

On the left arise
Huge, massy ramparts of eternal cliff,
Ragged and steep, with many a green recess
And fissure dark: Across the creek, upon
The swift slope of the mountain's jagged side,
Spread out the solemn groves wide-branched and dim
As old Cathedrals. But right on in front
The frowning perpendicular of rock
Expands, mid clustering festoons of thick leaves,
Into a noble vestibule, whose walls
Rise in an arched and adamantine dome.
Like a large, lustrous eye of blue, the sky
Looks in a blessing through the parted roof.

[1] "The Stone Church" is a natural curiosity of much celebrity, situated in a gorge of the mountains in Dover, Dutchess County, N. Y.

On 'neath the Gothic portal do we pass,
Up the dim aisle, above the dashing fall,
Whose white spray softens the melodious air,
'Till, passing thro' a narrow granite hall
We tread a spacious theatre of stone.
This is the Church. Its dædal walls are hung
As for a festival with laurel boughs,
With pendulous tresses of long moss and fern,
Bright tufts of grass, and sweet half buried flowers,
High crowned with gnarled and overleaning trees.
Dark, fallen cliffs are in the centre piled,
Most pulpit-like and stern. Swift from above
A silver cascade slides down to the floor,
With liquid syllables of lulling sound —
Chanting the hymn that Nature at its birth
Poured through its soft and music-loving lips.
Far over all, the sweet and tremulous sky
Bends its embracing canopy of love.

Here Nature seems at prayer ; and as you gaze
On her lone altar mid the list'ning hills,
And hear the ceaseless symphonies that float
From woods and waters on the cool sweet air,
You feel that holier aspirations steal
Into the willing heart — your subtler thought,
Tranced in the Benediction brooding round,
Glows half inspired with its unuttered praise.

1851.

PEWAUKEE.

THE blackbirds are wooing,
Reed-warblers are cooing,
The marsh-hens are chatt'ring and scolding away;
The young leaves are gleaming
In the soft sunshine streaming
From the blue, tender heaven of blossoming May.
Pewaukee! Pewaukee!
O lovely Pewaukee!
We hasten to greet thee, this beautiful day.

The black-bass are leaping
Where the still pools are sleeping,
And the birds, in the reeds, trill their operas o'er:
While over us hover,
Like the breath of a lover,
The odors of apple-boughs white on the shore.
Pewaukee, Pewaukee!
Delicious Pewaukee!
We hail thee, and love thee, and taste thee once more.

THE NEW EPOCH.

THE air is pained with war's confusing thunder;
The banners of great kingdoms are unfurled;
And fearful signs, and sights of awe and wonder,
Startle the vision of a gazing world.

On conquering hosts and armies torn and flying,
Through Rhenish hamlets and Gaul's gallant lines,
Beyond the Alps, where Papal Rome is dying,
To Hungary's hills and rough Iberia's vines,

Beneath the smoke of Albion's giant labors,
In cot, and mart, and stifling factory-pen,
A spirit swifter than the flash of sabres,
Now smites with light the expectant hearts of men.

Teuton and Gaul, wrong not the cause ye favor;
Loving the right, in amity embrace.
The sacrifice of Peace, with sweetest savor,
Shall rise approved to Heaven's applauding face.

Strong in the knowledge that the Truth discloses,
Soldiers of Prussia, be no longer dumb.
Your hire is earned: Enwreathe your guns with roses,—
Make FATHERLAND the freeman's lasting home.

O beauteous France, from crumbled thrones up-springing,
The hope of ages glittering on thy brow,
The bells of gladness through the earth are ringing
Loud gratulations o'er thy latest vow.

O Britain, quivering with strong aspirations,
Monarchs are weak when toiling millions rise;
Salute the young Republic; calm the nations;
In thy own people's wisdom thou art wise.

Amid the sheaves of Freedom's ample sowing,
Columbia bids the empires to her feast.
Toward man as *man* her mighty heart is flowing,
Like ocean-tides that bathe the West and East.

She knows the pain, the weariness, the weeping,
The darkness ere the child of peace is born.
"Europe," she cries, "thine may be glorious reaping
In fields now tangled by the briar and thorn.

"Unbind the chains that fester on the lowly,
O'erturn the thrones that grind God's helpless poor;
No rule is right, no power is just and holy,
That on a prostrate spirit shuts the door.

"Dead forms are chaff, fit only for the burning,
The craft of kings and priests has ruled too long.
O valiant millions spurred with noble yearning,
The time is ripe to crush the ancient Wrong.

"Grander than martial triumphs is the rending
Of tyrant scepters from polluted hands;
More glorious than imperial shows, the blending
Of peaceful standards o'er enfranchised lands."

O living hearts that surge against each other,
Until the turf with bloody flowers is red,
The man that fronts you is a friend and brother;
Smite hideous shapes, that curse the earth, instead —

Th' Errors nursed in Ignorance's dominions,
Dark Fears that haunt the mediæval cell,
Wrongs hatched beneath foul Superstition's pinions,
And all the sneaking, brutish brood of Hell.

But brother man to brother man be dearer!
  The cross and wormwood are not known in vain.
By every heart-throe thou art lifted nearer
  The royal day of Love's triumphant reign.

The Dawn already on the hills is tender;
  The Portents gleam of that prophetic time,
When all earth's flags, one stream of woven splendor,
  O'er a united race shall wave sublime!

1870.

A HYMN FOR 1861.

ALMIGHTY LORD, accept our praise.
  In Thee all creatures live and move,
The Ages, to the latest days,
  Repeat the story of Thy love.
We bless the Light that flows from Thee —
God save this land of Liberty!

Thy hand led forth our Patriot Sires;
  Our Nation by Thy counsels grew;
Stir up, we pray, the sacred fires
  Of Freedom in our breasts anew.
Thy Truth alone has made us free.
God save this land of Liberty!

Our homes and hearths in Thee are dear,
  By Thee our folds and fields increase,
This Vine of Thine own planting, rear,
  And fill with lasting fruits of Peace.
No weapon prospers aimed at Thee.
God save this land of Liberty!

Fold our broad realm in Thy embrace,
  Thy frown to foreign foes reveal,

And, in the sunshine of Thy face,
  The Nation's heart with Union seal.
The people cry from sea to sea,
"God save this land of Liberty!"

TO WILLIAM CULLEN BRYANT.

ON HIS SEVENTIETH BIRTHDAY.

THY patient feet have reached to-day
The allotted goal of human years;
Thanks, thanks to Him who bids thee stay
Awhile, yet, from the timeless spheres.

Thanks for thy journey brave and long;
A glorious pathway has it been,
Melodious with majestic song,
And hallowed in the hearts of men.

Earth's face is dearer for thy gaze.
The fields that thou hast travelled o'er
Are fuller blossomed, and the ways
Of toil more pleasant than before.

The April pastures breathe more sweet,
The brooks in deeper musings glide,
Old woodlands grander hymns repeat,
And holier seems the Autumn-tide.

The crystal founts and Summer rains
  Are haunted now with pictured grace ;
The winds have learned more tender strains,
  And greet us with more kind embrace.

More meekly pleads each flow'ret's eye,
  On gentler errands comes the snow,
And birds write on the evening sky
  More gracious lessons, as they go.

The stars, the clouds, the sea, the grave,
  Wide prairie wastes and crowded marts,
All that is fair, and good, and brave,
  In peaceful homes and gen'rous hearts,

Through thee their wond'rous meanings tell ;
  And as men go to work and pray —
Feeling thy song's persuasive spell —
  Love's face seems closer o'er their way.

Before thee Error howled and fled ;
  And in thy path, though bold and strong,
Oppression quailed. From thy hand sped
  The glittering shafts that crippled Wrong.

And thy lips swelled the thrilling peal
  That roused the people to uphold
The sacred cause of common weal.
  Oh may thy happy eyes behold

Fair Freedom's triumph, and the sway
  Of Peace, which after strife and pain,
Shall usher the illustrious day
  Of a great Nation born again!

Smooth be thy latest stages here,
  Revered, and loved, and watched by those
To whom thou seemest still more dear,
  The further on thy journey goes.

And keeping yet the child-like heart —
  Pure home of every sacred guest —
At last, in perfect peace, depart,
  O Bryant, to thy blissful rest.

1864.

THE TEMPTATION OF CHRIST.

A PICTURE BY ARY SCHEFFER.

MESSIAH and the Tempter face to face —
The Son of God and the Incarnate Fiend !
High on a cliff that cleaves the cold, thin air,
A bare, bleak, granite pinnacle that holds
Eternal friendship with the silent sky,
Above the mighty kingdoms stand the twain.
Oh ! how unlike their office and estate,
Their aspects, aims, ambitions, essences.
Celestial and infernal attributes confront,
Upon whose awful issues now depend
Extreme of good or evil unto man.
August, serene, like the repose of God,
Save in the mortal sorrows of his face,
Which the immortal sweetens and subdues,
Stands the Redeemer. His benignant brow,
Though pallid with austerities and pain,
Wears sweet compassion, and his lifted arm
Points, with unconscious grandeur, to his throne
Beyond the azure. In his patient eyes,
Deep, dark, divine, unutterably calm,
Swim solemn visions of old prophecies —

His trials, toils, and triumphs yet to come:
These shade their tender depths, where love and truth
Keep gen'rous audience; turning not in scorn
E'en from this subtle embassy of sin.
Poised but a step below, Hell's winged King,
Half suppliant, half in arrogant suspense,
Looks upward in this climax of affront.
There is no human malice on his face,
No maniac frenzy throttling its result;
But doubt, fear, hope, and hate, sublimed and fused
Into the direst instincts of revenge;
And the mature conclusions of a soul
Spurred by the bitter shame of old defeat,
And wrathful resolution wrung from woe,
Keen-edged and tempered by relentless will.
Oh! in the steadfast fervor of his glare,
His treacherous game half seems divine intent,
And his proud head and self-reliant front
Suggest the sphery splendor of his prime.
With downward pointing gesture hear him speak—
(Audacious venture of a desperate hope),
"*All these great kingdoms and their royalties,*
If thou wilt kneel and worship me, are thine."

A VISION.

Before me rose a realm
Silent, and vast, and vague with shapes unborn,
Which fiery hands, with fateful force, did whelm
Ere dawned the natal morn.

Myriads whose pulses beat
Delicious tune with the maternal blood,
Struck where Love's trusts are most divinely sweet,
Sank in the shoreless flood.

The frailest frames of man,
Faint embryo forms that held the soul in place,
Dim miniatures of all that fills the plan
Of the great human race.

What might have been, I said,
Had these pale buds but come to Nature's flower;
What perfect fruits from royal boughs been shed —
The ages' golden dower!

What stalwart sons of light,
Regal with Wisdom's scepter and its crown,

What daughters making Love's dominion bright
With virginal renown!

What lips of glorious speech,
What clear-browed sovereigns o'er Thought's choiring spheres,
What valiant hands to guard the Right, and reach
The prize of waiting years!

What souls to take the morn
Of God's great glory in their eager eyes,
And, trampling down all baseness with swift scorn,
To Duty's summits rise!

What that is fair and true—
Beauty whose splendors awe profane caress-
Imperial natures that exhale the dew
Of marvelous loveliness.

What that might not have grown
To lordliest stature, grand in heart and brain,
Bequeathing gifts that flash from zone to zone
An unextinguished flame.

Victims of cruel doom,
What are they, or what not, in that strange deep,
Where smitten, birthless, falls the leaden gloom
Of their mysterious sleep?

Shall cold oblivion fold
Her pall forever o'er this countless host?
Or shall they yet, with starry Angels, hold
The crowns their mothers lost?

THE RIVER OF TEARS.

In the ghastly dusk of cypress shade
O'er the beaten sands of a dismal glade,
The River of Tears, with ceaseless flow,
Rolls its bitter waves of human woe.

The herbless mountains that gird the vale,
In an endless dawn, stand cold and pale;
And the lustreless clouds droop down so low,
They touch the face of the stream below.

No honeyed blossoms breathe balm around
In the funeral gloom that shrouds the ground;
But dark, rank weeds reach greedily o'er
To sip the surge on the level shore.

Wild shrieks oft startle the dusky air,
And the smothered howl of mad despair, —
While the pleading wail of love's last cry
Floats o'er the waves to the leaden sky.

In aimless courses deep footprints go,
Of the suffering ones of long ago, —
As the sad procession, with claspéd hands,
Went wandering over the barren sands.

In the sullen shadows brooding here,
Stalk pallid Sorrow and shivering Fear,
Frail Youth, bent Age, and the bad and bold,
And the gentle and good whose lives grew cold.

In hopeless anguish some hide their eyes,
And with pale, wan looks, some watch the skies,
Some beat their bosoms with frenzied stare,
And some feel round in the empty air.

Thus in mournful groups they come and go,
None tells to another his weight of woe;
And the swollen stream, 'neath the dusky shroud,
Goes down to its sea of noiseless cloud.

MOSSES.

In this lone spot of weedy mould,
  Watched by no sad, regretful eyes,
Mid matted herbage damp and cold,
  An old forgotten grave-stone lies.

A briar's thorny fingers keep
  Each piece of broken slab apart,
And ancient mosses darkly sleep
  On all its wealth of lettered art.

Here once were graven names and dates,
  Affections, titles, triumphs, trust ;
All that memorial Love relates
  To grace the mute abandoned dust.

Beneath each green oblivious lid
  What treasuries of sorrow lie,
In cankering rust forever hid,
  While all the great world jostles by.

I linger, though the night is drear,
  And each cloud shoots a fiery dart;
For sympathy begets no fear,
  And moss is heavy on my heart !

The briars of anguish pierce and fold
 Each broken trust, and many a weed
Chokes up the warm and generous mould,
 Where I had planted golden seed.

How many tender records, traced
 In flowery rhyme on scrolls of white,
Sweet names with gilded wreath enchased,
 There moulder, buried from the sight.

And o'er Joy's empty fountain trail
 Dead lilies, spreading suppliant palms,
And withered passion-flowers, pale
 With pleading for Affection's alms.

Oh, down these moss-grown ruins rest
 Sealed treasuries of hope and tears ;
There Love folds on his bloodless breast
 The cold dreams of departed years.

There Memory o'er the falsely fair
 Sleeps with her web across her eyes,
And Fancy, palsied with despair,
 Waves no bright pinion in the skies.

O Heart ! what records strange ye keep,
 While round life's rosy currents flow ;
But bury thy pale orphans deep,
 And still smile on, none care to know.

WONOMSCOPOMIC.[1]

THE dainty ripples lisping summer speech,
  Tease pearly blossoms nestling near the shore ;
On slopes of sunshine robins sit and teach,
  In undertones, the happy air their lore.
A purple cloud hung in voluptuous blue
  Waits for some mystic message from the pines ;
Shades drowse sweet nooks, and odors wanton through
  The glossy ringlets of luxuriant vines.

Their golden bosoms leaning round and round,
  The harvest fields a ripe contentment know ;
Through ancient groves and o'er low meadow ground
  A murmurous gladness ever seems to flow.
Far off the circling mountains stand and doze,
  With vistas opening into shimmering haze,
And the low clouds, which on bald peaks repose,
  Seem like the fire of some half-smothered blaze.

[1] The Indian name of a beautiful lake in Salisbury, Connecticut.

Before me, in this quiet, sleeps the lake,
  Like some pure heart where heaven deep-mirrored lies,
And still so winning that its friendships make
  All that *it* loves more lovely in our eyes.
I muse along the margin, where the joy
  Of Beauty thrilled me with delicious pain ;
But deeper in my heart than when a boy,
  Streams the calm glory of the scene again.

A SUNSET AT LONGMONT, COLORADO.

WE'VE journeyed through the mountains. There
they stand
Broad-based, majestic in a grand repose,
Some three leagues westward. Longmont wel-
comes us;
And while we rest this balmy Summer eve
At hospitable thresholds, all the sky,
As if to consecrate our holiday,
And make our precious memories more dear,
Puts on unwonted glory; and our eyes,
Like those of Moses in the mount, are smit
With sudden splendor. For the sinking sun
Hidden, is not repressed, but pours its light
Upward and far aslant on flocks of cloud,
Along the clear horizon's narrow rim,
Down the great gulfs of everlasting rock,
O'er shining peaks, the distant Snowy Range,
And Long's high crown, while all the nearer hills
In tender shadow watch the miracle.
Spread to the right, and gleaming fold on fold,
Vermilion, saffron, pink, and pearly white,
The gorgeous banners of the clouds are flung,
Waving and tossing in resplendent surge,

Above yon belt of deep delicious sky,
Whose liquid opal perfect, passionless,
Runs to a field of luminous em'rald,
Broidered with marv'lous fringe of crimson fire.
More southward fleecy draperies touched with rose
Float on the air, and here and there droop low
Upon the shoulders of the purple peaks.
O'erhead the arrows of the hidden sun
Flash, now and then, on cliffs of ragged cloud ;
And plumes of radiance, like strange tropic birds,
Flit through the open spaces of the blue.
High up amid the awful gaps of rock,
Between the ranges, a soft sea of bloom —
The lustrous pollen of this sunset-flower —
Throbs wave on wave against the granite shore.
Wondrous the billows of this golden mist,
Sweet, tender, lucent, as if purest dews
Of Paradise had washed the starry sheen
From heaven's choicest blossoms, and poured all
Into the porphyry basin of the mount,
A perfect incense to the unseen God.
Unasked we join the worship of the hour,
Breathless with indescribable applause.
The sacred spell of Beauty on us lies,
And Power that dwells in Light's essential throne,
And Love in which all that is good is born.
The curtains of the glowing deep are drawn,
And through the vista garlanded with gold,

O'er amethystine herbage, lawns of rose,
Pure streams where lilies of the Angels blow,
Far toward the sightless glory of the Lord,
Our hearts are borne in utterless content,
Renewed and resting on the Infinite!

AMENIA.

A PLEASANT vale; bright fields that lie
  On gentle slopes and knolls of green;
Steep mountains sharp against the sky;
  Clear streams and tiny lakes between.

Cool bowery lanes 'mong happy hills;
  Old groves that shade ancestral eaves;
Farms which the prosperous season fills
  With flocks, and fruits, and golden sheaves.

A holy feeling soothes the air,
  The woodlands stand in the musings sweet,
It seems as if the heart of prayer
  In all this charméd valley beat.

The hills are voiced with sacred speech,
  The meadows bloom with sweet desire,
From mountains kindred spirits reach
  To clasp the glory streaming higher.

In every path I see the trace
  Of feet that made the landscape dear;
In every flower I feel the grace
  Of lives that purely blossomed here.

The robins, at the homestead gate,
 Rehearse the radiant dreams of May ;
Fair faces at the windows wait ; —
 With love's warm breath the curtains sway.

The Sabbath bell its message sends,
 Which climbs the sky with silvery feet ;
Upon the little church descends
 And broods the Blessed Paraclete.

O halcyon days, when happy eyes
 Undimmed by doubt, or care, or tears,
Saw life in mystic beauty rise,
 And ripen through the joyous years.

O hearts to noble impulse true,
 In mutual faith and purpose strong,
Refreshed with love's celestial dew,
 And leaping to the voice of song!

Spring through the summer cannot stay;
 Some flowers unfold not in our sun ;
Some fruit falls ere the Autumn day ;
 Through purging fires the gold is won.

Loved homes grow vacant year by year,
 New graves are green, old paths untrod,
But still AMENIA grows more dear,
 Embosomed in the smile of God!

TO WILLIAM F. COOLBAUGH.

ON HIS BIRTHDAY.

Like one who waits 'neath an embowering vine,
On some green cliff that looks upon the sea,
And far away o'er mountain, vale, and lea,
Where the enchantment to his senses fine —
The subtile charm of Nature's sacred wine —
Breathes joy, and awe, and tender mystery;
So thou, to-day, confronting all thy years,
Dost view the landscape which thy heart endears —
Youth's rosy fields and skies with promise set,
Paths that in manhood led to fair renown,
And holy graves with memory's dew-drops wet,
Care's rugged steeps, and Labor's splendid crown.
What pageants pass! what hands are waved afar!
How strangely sweet the ancient voices are!

Thy household treasures show their dimless gold;
Young faces look in thine, and young lips teach
Thy heart life's sweetest truths in songful speech;
Home's peerless Flower festoons the new and old.

Thanks to thy helpful hand and tireless brain,
The graces learned in friendship's gentle school,
The wisdom that can cheer, and guide, and rule,
The spirit that in virtue reckons gain.
How many barques are wrecked whose pennons flew
In softer airs than ever favored thine!
Rough seas or fair, our way is always through
The unknown deep; but fadeless landscapes shine
For him whose life is freighted with the store
Of that which thrives on the immortal shore.

1875

THE GREEK SLAVE.

A STATUE BY HIRAM POWERS.

A FETTERED girl on alien sands,
With homeless heart and aching feet.
'T would seem that Slavedom's iron bands
Would crumble from a thing so sweet.

A blameless virgin. How the crowd
Gaze wond'ring in the market-place,
As if Aurora, from a cloud
Of glory, met them face to face!

Robed in her spirit's spotless white,
From evil eyes she stands secure.
There cannot, in the sacred light
That spheres her, breathe a thought impure.

What golden isle, mid purple seas,
Nursed into bloom a shape so rare?
In Paphos or the Cyclades
Did her warm beauty flush the air?

Did Lesbian odors steep her dreams
  Till life became a roseate trance?
Did Dian, by Laconian streams,
  Teach her the woodland's chaste romance?

O pure young face, whose drooping eyes
  Veil not a dream of earthly stain,
What pensive sorrow on thee lies?
  What patient strength and silent pain?

Perhaps memorial fancies come —
  The pictured joys of childhood's hour;
Thoughts of the long, sweet days of home,
  As blossomed life's delicious flower.

Perhaps o'er seas, a weary dove,
  Her heart goes pining for its mate;
Or hears the voice of 'wildered love
  Far off bemoan her dismal fate.

Perhaps, not utterly forlorn,
  Her quenchless hopes go up the sky,
And, like faint stars amid the morn,
  In Heaven's serene effulgence lie.

O triumph of prophetic Art!
  Wronged human kind appeals in thee:
When shall Force cease to bruise the heart,
  And earth from sordid lust be free?

In thy repose of suffering dwells
  A faith that sees through time and fear:
We gaze till on the future wells
  The joy of Freedom's perfect year.

TO WILLIAM CULLEN BRYANT,

ON HIS EIGHTIETH BIRTHDAY.

THE sweetest blossoms any bring
  To-day to deck thy Muse's throne
Are those that out of pure hearts spring,
  From seed thy fruitful life has sown.

How deep thy living thought struck down
  In countless souls throughout the land;
The splendid flowers of thy renown
  In myriad leaves of light expand.

They bloom in virtues strong and true,
  In deeds that make our kinship sweet,
Chaste homes and lives of spotless hue,
  In Love that serves with tireless feet;

In patriot zeal; in Honor's breast;
  Where Duty runs without debate;
Where Nature feasts her reverent guest,
  And Faith waits calmly "at the Gate."

These garlands of the spirit live,
  While festal splendors pass away ;
Millions their fadeless tribute give
  To thee, O kingly Bard, to-day.

Thanks for thy pure, majestic song,
  Thy golden years' o'ermeasured span,
Thy valiant will to smite the wrong,
  Thy vast unconquered love of man.

Thanks for thy simple faith and truth ;
  Thanks for thy wisdom, deep and calm,
The freshness of thy generous youth,
  Thy life — a sweet, triumphant psalm !

Earth's children catch its strains sublime
  As ages bear along thy name,
And down the glowing fields of time
  The wise and good reflect thy fame.

MEMORIAL DAY.

OUT of thine azure depths, O sun benign!
Shower thy golden kisses on the May:
Drink, fertile fields, kind Nature's mystic wine,
Till every herb throb with a life divine,—
Let not a single dew-drop go astray.
Brood, moistened airs, with warm and fragrant wing,
On all the vales, and haste with glowing feet,
Ye soft-lipped Hours, to make the landscape sweet,
Till earth shall burst to flowers — a perfect spring!
O vernal season! give your richest blooms —
Rare radiance woven in celestial looms,
The subtlest meanings of each tint and tone
That Beauty keeps about her peerless throne;
Our hearts ache with unsyllabled applause.
We are unworthy, but for those who lie
In graves made holy by their life-blood shed —
The hero youth who took our periled cause,
And thought it sweet and beautiful to die,
That Freedom's fields be by us harvested,—
We crave the choicest emblems to impart
The sense of that which blossoms in the heart.

Even then how meagre is our speech to breathe
Our thanks, our praise, our love, our joyous pride: —
Seraphic hands alone are fit to wreathe
Chaplets for those who kissed our flag and died.
O sacred dust! O precious seed, that bears
The blessed fruits that make a people strong, —
Life out of death; Right victor over Wrong.
We bow to Him who wisely smites and spares,
Who gives the spirit that endures and dares,
The love of man and the heroic will.
He is the Lord, our Strength and Refuge still!
The nation lives. After war's bloody showers,
The air is sweet with Freedom's stainless flowers.
Let praise ascend and gratulations grand,
The graves of martyrs consecrate the land.
O shrines of duty! Honor's deathless urns!
By you more deep our patriot ardor burns.
The gates are lifted of the historic years: —
Lo! musterings, partings, watchings, sudden fears,
The march, the fiery charge, the loved and slain,
Foul prison pens, and all the hope and pain
Of war's suspense, our prayers, the welcome word
That smote the bondsman's fetters like a sword,
Our Lincoln dead! — what pictures rise and rise,
Until the tears well up from heart to eyes,

And then with light across our future gleaming,
    Rainbows of promise beautiful and bright
Span all the years, and all the sky is streaming
    With Union banners, red and blue and white;
The Truth is strong: God will defend the right!

CHARLES H. RAY.

I WAS writing a poem of freedom,
  And I thought, as the verses grew,
One, at least, will look on them kindly,
  Who knows well the ring of the true ; —

One who loves the Right, and is bravest
  When the weak need help from the strong —
He will feel the thrill of the lyric,
  And throb with the hope of the song.

At evening the poem was finished ;
  I awoke with the day, and read
Of him, whose life was so precious,
  " The patriot thinker is dead."

And the light went out of the morning,
  For its weeping I thanked the rain,
The very trees through the city,
  And the dumb streets seemed to complain.

And I wondered that men could traffic,
  Or talk to each other aloud,
While the heart so great and tender
  Was pulseless and cold in its shroud ; —

The heart that, with aching and yearning,
Had bled through a tireless pen,
That, in labors of love and duty,
At last burnt itself out for men.

But I knew that in city and country
There was sobbing a grief like mine,
In souls that his spirit had strengthened,
Like giants refreshed with new wine.

And there seemed to my vision unfolded,
As a scroll illumined and vast,
The words he had written for freedom,
The hope on the age he had cast.

And I read with a strong consolation ;
While his life seemed speaking to mine,
"The good that is wrought is eternal ;
To labor for man is divine."

And the earth grew brighter and brighter,
And the sun came after the rain :
True Heart ! thy service was noble,
Rest, rest, after struggle and pain.

September 24, 1870.

THE LAND OF DESPAIR.

Between an endless, shipless strand,
And mountains peaked in icy air —
One sunless, cheerless waste of sand —
Stretch the bleak regions of Despair.

The red horizon's sullen brim
Dips round the scowling, twilight sea,
Where sheeted phantoms, swift and dim,
Before some viewless Presence flee.

The cold steeps, on the other hand,
Gape with black caves and gulfs profound,
And like huge frozen cloud-racks stand,
O'ershadowing all the dismal ground.

No fountain hath the waste, no fruit.
No blossoms scent the heavy breeze;
But here and there, barked to the root,
Lean the gaunt wrecks of blasted trees.

A hungry vulture, on a rift
Of splintered granite, glares for prey;
And a few ravens slowly drift
Through the dull air, and pass away.

Here dwell the fierce, the foul, the frail,
  The demon-eyed with tangled hair,
The weak, the sadly worn and pale,
  The stony-browed, who once were fair.

Some rave beside the mocking sea ;
  Some toss the sands ; some crouch in caves ;
Some, stabbed with mighty agony,
  Are ever digging useless graves.

Imprisoned, hopeless, tortured, curst,
  In vain they moan, and gasp, and pray
The blank skies, with a thunder burst,
  To sweep their withered lives away.

A MURMUR OF MAY.

I AM cropping the violets to-day in the meadows,
Where in childhood I gathered them blameless as they:
The birds in the sunshine float singing around me,
And heaven is over me tender with May.

I am waiting to-day by the streamlet, which prattles
And laughs through the vale, as it glides to the sea; —
The same happy brooklet that, in my bright Springtime,
So charmed me with stories of what I should be.

I am straying to-day mid the orchard, whose odors
Touched my heart with an exquisite rapture when young: —
The blossoms, and robins, and gladness of children,
Make a poem more perfect than ever was sung.

I am musing to-day where the fresh grass is growing
On mounds that were not when my summers were few,
And the violets, the brook, and the apple boughs bring me
All the sweetness and sadness I have tasted life through.

TO ROBERT COLLYER.

I MISS thy face, dear friend, thy voice, thy hand, —
  Thy rugged face through which the clear soul shines,
  Thy voice, now plaintive as the moan of pines,
And then a trumpet mighty in command;
Thy honest palm, whose grasp all understand.
  Though pleasant be the places where the lines
  Are fallen to me, yet my heart repines
Oft for the gardens of that goodly land
  Where our souls wandered, when they haply met,
With yearnings strong for man's diviner day,
  And landscapes blossomed, which no tears could wet,
Till old things, fit to perish, passed away,
  And life to God's great harmony was set,
And Love was monarch with unhindered sway.

IN THE MORNING.

IN THE MORNING.

IN THE LANE.

THE roses lingering in the west,
Soft lustre swooning through the sky,
The meadow blossoms kissed to rest,
A dying bird song floating by.

Old dusky woodlands soothed with balm
On mountains hushed in twilight trance,
The glossy eve's delicious calm,
Drowsed by the stream's voluptuous dance.

The soft dew silvering hawthorn bloom,
Faint crimson buds along the ledge, —
Two faces in the tender gloom
Between the lindens and the hedge ;

Two beamy faces young and sweet,
Cheek meeting cheek in tenderest trust,

White garlands strewn by waiting feet,
  And fire-flies showering golden dust.

They made in this familiar place
  The sweet completion Nature sought,
And all the scene's divinest grace
  Perfection from their beauty caught.

There were no vows nor splendid speech
  To break love's tranced and golden dream ;
Heart flowed as truly each to each
  As in one channel stream with stream.

There in the May's embalmed repose,
  Fair as if always nursed with May,
Their red lips flushing in one rose,
  Whose sweetness in each bosom lay,

They seemed the perfect dream that steals,
  At times, adown life's morning sky,
And, for one blessed hour, reveals
  The joy that haunts us till we die.

Like silvered raven-down, the dark
  Kept floating through the hawthorn lane,
And still the fire-fly's lustrous spark
  Fell on the dusk like amber rain.

A tremor through the daisied grass,
  A murmur like a happy bird,

A low bough bent for one to pass,
  And all as if no leaf had stirred.

The silvery dusk along the lane,
  Kept stealing by the creamy hedge,
And felt for those warm lips in vain,
  Clear to the runlet's lilied edge.

Gone through the shadows — nevermore
  With cheek to cheek they hither came ;
The great world crushes on, and o'er
  Its sweetest blossoms leaves no name.

THE FISHER BOY.

A STATUE BY HIRAM POWERS.

MOULDED in pure and perfect grace,
His white feet poised on silent sands,
And boyhood's spirit on his face,
A shape of life's best hour he stands.

His net droops on the idle oar,
He listens, as to whispers dear, —
What hears he on the mighty shore,
Pressing the sea-shell to his ear?

It is the soft-toned rapture caught
From rosy lips of Naiades,
That brims, with pictured joy, his thought
Of the rare beauty of the seas?

Is it some loved, unuttered name,
Wooed by the waves from lands remote,
Or echo of forgotten fame,
Kept in the shell's vermilion throat?

Or some strange syllables he seeks,
  Of ancient ocean's mystic lore, —
The solemn measures that she speaks
  With charmed tongues forevermore?

Still listening in that keen suspense,
  What curious fancies come and go;
What pleasant wishes thrill his sense
  For what he ne'er, ah, ne'er shall know!

O Artist! in whose deathless thought
  This radiant being lived and grew,
More glorious meaning hast thou wrought,
  Than thy divine conception knew!

For 't is the type of Youth's rich trance,
  Beside the wide World's unknown sea,
Weaving the sweet tones of romance
  Into the promised bliss to be:

Of Youth, that on life's golden brim,
  Hears many a sweet, mysterious strain,
And by, sees splendid visions swim,
  It ne'er shall meet, to love again:

Youth, yet all freshness — frail and fair —
  Whose tender trusts and loving will,
Ere chilled by scorn, or scarred by care,
  All time with speechless glory fill.

LILIES.

GRACEFULLY poised on bended knee,
In nature's sweet simplicity,
The maiden reaches a pearly hand
Where the spotless water-lilies stand.

'Tis a deep, still pool where the lilies blow
In a cluster that gleams like a wave of snow.
The pool is a mirror clear and fair,
How beautiful is the maiden there!

The place is full of lovely things,
The region with morning light is drowned,
Great, ruddy blossoms and golden wings
A fairy lustre sprinkle round.

The hidden brooks and songful birds
Make richer melody than words;
And bowery nooks, on flowery ground,
In odors subtler than sound
Breathe welcomes warm, and soft, and sweet.
The very mosses coax the feet
To linger on their silken ease;

With perfumed lips the zephyrs tease
The heart with all that heart can please.
Already there begins to shine
The luscious fruit on tree and vine.

The maiden has cropped the lilies white,
In the amber glow of morning light;
The maiden has cropped the lilies, why
Do the gaudier flowers not win her eye?
Why sports she not in the fairy dell?
Why yields she not to the witching spell?
Why gives she not, in the charming place,
The dew and bloom of her maiden grace?
Ah! vain these thralls — she has her prize:
The virgin flower in her bosom lies.
On, on, she hastes, while voices say
From all bright things deliciously,
"O maiden stay, oh stay,
Thy white-leaved lilies cast away,
Pass here the beauty of thy May."

The path is stern where she fain would go
With heart uplift and face aglow,
The path is rough and rises high,
Where the cold wind sweeps from an austere sky;
But more and more deliciously
The choir of tempting voices say,
"O maiden stay, oh stay,
Thy white-leaved lilies cast away,

This is the Happy Land for aye."
She hears, but will not heed the call, —
If she loses the lilies, she loses all.
Closer she presses the stainless prize,
With the light of faith in her liquid eyes,
And fearless she threads the narrow way,
That leads to the dawn of the perfect Day.

A WINTER REVERIE.

It is the middle of the night;
The patient stars with solemn march
Move up their grand triumphal arch,
The moon is cold and ghastly white.

I hear afar the muffled brook,
It murmurs one continuous name;
I read of glory, power, and fame,
But see one image in my book.

She sleeps, the beautiful, the true,
And soft-winged dreams with sweet surprise
Unfold their pictures to her eyes,
And fill her panting heart anew.

She knows not how my fancies frame
A thousand garlands for her now,
And how with love, lips ne'er avow,
I whisper o'er and o'er her name.

She thinks not in her dreamy rest
That eyes are tearful for her sake,
That busy memories are awake,
And longings haunt the anxious breast.

Oh, gentle Soother! poppied Sleep!
    Breathe softly on her lids of snow,
    And as the angels come and go,
Enchanted watches round her keep.

THE ANGEL IN THE MOON.

She leaned against the window, her fair hair
Thrown from her brow, her eyes in azure trance
Bent on the sky, and her rare lips by thought
Pressed half apart. The lustrous moonlight lay
Upon her lucid neck, and through its sheen,
That strove to drown her beauty, rose bloom shone
From her Aurorian cheek. Hushed as a star
Seen in some silver wave, she stood amid
The tranquil splendor; and our little room
Seemed like the entrance to an altar place.
Soon with calm gesture, pointing to the moon,
She beckoned me, and with a voice, which fell
Upon the breathless glory, like a song
Flung from cherubic lips on bowers which bloom
By Life's bright river, said, "An Angel, lo!
A glorious Angel blazes in the moon!"
Where she saw the celestial one I gazed,
But turned away unblest. With tiny hand,
Whose taper fingers thrilled with secret joy,
Again she led my wandering vision there,
Upon the silver ladder of the light —
Still talking of the Angel, as it lay

Within the calmness of the moon's deep smile.
She told me of its beauty — how its wings
Were slanting towards the azure — how its robes
In wavy grace streamed on the colored air —
Of its bright arm bent through the billowy glow
That heaved around its shoulders — its deep eyes,
Full of immortal transports — and its brow
Fresh with the dazzling radiance of Heaven.
I saw it not; but as I turned and gazed
Upon the form beside me — like a saint
Tranced in a golden vision, crowned and bathed
With halos of the moonlight — and then thought
Of her pure, guileless heart, and tender youth,
Fresh with sweet hope and beauty, like the dawn
Over Idalean gardens — I believed
It was quite useless thus to scan the moon,
When such an Angel stood and talked with me.

A LESSON FROM THE SKY.

THE sun is set, and still as Time
The great sky broods benign and calm ;
Neglected like some ancient rhyme,
I stand and wonder that I am !

Athwart the portals of the west
One fiery cloud slopes still and stern,
While waking from delicious rest,
A trembling star begins to burn.

The glory of the western throne
By yon red arm is guarded now ;
O young heart ! toiling here alone,
What to the world's great strength art thou ?

But lo ! I see the star-urn pour
Its soothing light beyond the skies,
While pale as sand-ribs on the shore,
The shrunken cloud in darkness lies.

Young heart — be strong ! for thee the star
In heaven's serene and tender deep :
The world's dread arm thy course may bar, —
It wastes with every watch ye keep.

1853.

SONG.

AN IMITATION.

THE icicles hang in the forest
Over the blacksand rocks,
And snow-drifts beneath the hedges
Are sleeping like white flocks.
Is your bosom warm to-night, Lilly?
Can your soft eyes find the light, Lilly?
I think of your face with its golden locks:
Oh, God shield thee — shield thee, my Lilly,
For I can save never more!

No moonlight gushes its silver
Into the leafless wood,
Blossoms are froze in the fountains,
Where hand in hand we stood;
Where come your young dreams now, Lilly?
Who kisses your fair, pale brow, Lilly?
I walk in the dark of a deep solitude;
Oh, God bless thee — bless thee, my Lilly,
For I can bless never more!

The weird hollow winds keep moaning
Ever through glen, through wold —

Clouds marshal up from the ocean,
Scowling and black with cold;
Where linger your tender feet, Lilly?
Who feels your warm heart beat, Lilly?
Your fair white hands do the angels hold?
Oh, God love thee — love thee, my Lilly,
For I love thee evermore!

1853.

THE FOREST GRAVE.

AMONG the flowers far away,
In June's soft, slumberous air,
Beneath the wood's green canopies
They laid her, young and fair.

Alone beneath the trees she loved,
'Mid blossoms where she prayed,
And where her aching heart grew still
Her tender form was laid.

No maidens gazed on her sweet face,
And turned away to weep ;
No mother pressed a farewell kiss
As there she lay asleep.

Ah ! little knew the rough, stern men
That smoothed her bed of rest,
Of all the tender, tearful things
Hid in her silent breast.

THE STARS IN THE STREAM.

BETWEEN the steep and sunny hills
  That all the dreamy vale inclose,
With many a bright and graceful curve
  A clear and placid streamlet flows.
There soft, green banks slope gently down,
  And groups of fragrant trees bend o'er,
Fresh blossoms nestle in the grass,
  And shining pebbles gem the shore.

Here in the spiritual night,
  When all the glorious earth was still,
As if the hand of God was spread
  Above the deep woods of the hill,
A fair-faced boy, with deep blue eyes,
  And hair like sunlight's wavy beam,
Would come and sit for hours, and gaze
  Upon the thick stars in the stream.

He wondered why the golden stars,
  That hung so far amid the sky,
Should also in the wave below
  In such a trance of beauty lie.

And there for many a balmy night,
  He lingered by the silver shore, —
So innocent with dear desires,
  That questioned all things more and more.

A lonely, thoughtful boy was he,
  In love with all things good and fair,
Great hopes and wishes filled his heart,
  Before he hardly knew them there.
But still that heart grew bold and strong,
  That love more broad and earnest grew, —
He saw the inner sense of things,
  And Nature's mystic meanings knew.

Long years had passed since he reposed
  Upon the bank of that fair stream —
Long years of thought and holy toil
  Had taught him life was not a dream.
The same stars in the placid wave
  Wore still the same soft crowns of light,
And all along the banks, flowed down
  To his true heart the same delight.

He wondered not now they were there,
  So sweetly, tremulously bright,
Nor why star looked again to star
  From waters to the fields of light;
For he had learned that Love's own law
  Is to restore what it receives,

That each kind look and tender word
  Its image in the bosom leaves.

He wondered not that at his feet
  The space-born orbs so softly shone,
He knew the heart when turned to Heaven
  May make its starry joys its own ;
And that the more serenely pure
  That heart shall keep through day and night,
The more divine shall glow within
  The love-stars of celestial light.

1851.

YOU AND I.

SWEET longings hinted at and guessed,
Tender spiritual unrest —
We cannot near each other live,
Unless we something take and give —
You and I.

Playing with old regrets, we wait,
Half happy, half accusing Fate;
A broken Hope is like a ghost!
We both seek something we have lost —
You and I.

Not often may such natures meet,
So sweetly tender, subtly sweet;
The instincts of pure souls are just —
We *now* may know in whom we trust —
You and I.

The world is cold, the world is vain;
Apart, we both shall wear the chain.
Our griefs make each the other's guest;
Two hearts in one give perfect rest —
You and I.

A BIRTHDAY LYRIC.

LEAD me 'mong blossoms white
In the early amber light,
Away from teasing Care,
And let the charmèd air,
With luscious tone,
Soothe me with strains unknown.

Oh! heap the blossoms sweet
About my face and feet,
Till half the blushing sky,
And the nook wherein I lie,
Are curtained most deliciously.
With odors deluge me,
With rose-light and low melody; —
For I would dream, until earth seems
What once it promised in my dreams.

O radiant land! where my young eyes
Saw angels in the rainbow skies,
And felt Love's arms in all the air,
And heard Hope singing everywhere —
Sweet land of boyhood! Rose unblown!
Delicious heart-enfolded zone!

How soon — too soon!
The burning Noon
Drank all thy dew from bud and leaf,
And seared the bowers of Young Belief; —

The drifting sands before me spread
With murky redness overhead;
I faint with fighting wrong and sin;
To-day, oh, let me enter in
The gardens beautiful of yore,
And live again my May-life o'er.
I may come forth more firm and strong
To deal with error, blame, and wrong;
Upon my heart fresh dew shall lie,
And heaven seem nearer to mine eye.

AN EPITHALAMIUM.

I.

WAIT within this slumb'rous vale,
Here is always dreamful ease,
Od'rous noon and twilight pale
Mingle in the woven trees ;
Mountains heaving round and round
Sweeten ev'ry wandering air,
And the mazes of the ground
Witch the sense with welcomes rare :
Stay, oh stay, for only here
Life ripens through Love's perfect year.

II.

Wait upon this bow'ry shore,
Here is always sunny calm,
Muffled is the billows' roar
In the air's delicious balm ;
Every cloud holds visions sweet,
Even dew a rainbow brings,
Velvet blossoms coax the feet,
Overhead are shining wings :
Stay, oh stay, for only here
Life ripens through Love's perfect year.

III.

Wait amid this luscious isle,
  Here is always honeyed rest,
Ocean's garnered wealth of smile
  Lingers here a constant guest;
Gleaming grottoes gem the dells —
  Haunt of nymphs of olden time,
Every leaf a legend tells,
  Every echo murmurs rhyme:
Stay, oh stay, for only here
Life ripens through Love's perfect year.

AN AUTUMN PICTURE.

THE nook with Autumn's smile is gay.
 Soft sunshine glints the ancient rocks,
Sifts through bright boughs, in golden spray,
 Upon the sumach's crimson locks,

And paints quaint legends of the sky
 'Tween shadows of the grassy space.
September's wizard fingers tie
 Garlands of asters round the place,

And fringe the briery thicket's vest
 With drooping plumes of golden-rod.
With eyes that picture perfect rest
 The gentians look their thanks to God.

From one great oak a mighty vine
 Leaps to yon ledge of frosted ferns ;
Below, beside a whispering pine,
 A maple's scarlet turret burns.

Bowered within the sweet recess —
 Half in the sun and half in shade,
Rifling a hazel-bush's tress —
 A fair-cheeked boy and little maid.

He bends the fruitful branches low,
  So she the ripe, brown nuts may reach ;
And all the while, with hearts aglow,
  Together flows their joyous speech.

Their rosy hopes in music rise ;
  They tell their dreams of sweet desire ;
To them the world in sunshine lies —
  An Eden with no sword of fire

To guard the wondrous garden, where
  The fruits and flowers of every hue,
And witching sounds of od'rous air,
  Invite their feet to wander through.

O soul of youth ! O happy twain !
  In loving service blessing each, —
Both richer in each other's gain, —
  How deep the lesson that ye teach !

THE ARGOSY.

IN the emerald meadows,
  Below a leafy hill,
A child had launched his navy
  Of lilies on the rill;
A precious little argosy,
  Those lilies fresh and white;
As on the dancing waves they rode,
  He shouted with delight.

He watched their dainty beauty,
  As they gayly floated on,
Now toying round the velvet banks
  And rocking in the sun;
And then, like silver arrows
  In waves of winter light,
Aflashing down the foaming fall,
  And shooting out of sight.

The birds sang pæans o'er him,
  The sky was fragrant still,
Bright butterflies sailed round his ships,
  Soft winds crept from the hill;

His loose locks floated in the sun,
He warbled with the stream,
For life there, in the meadows,
Had the glory of a dream.

Beside a mighty river,
Where it meets the sounding main,
An old man saw his stately ships
Float off to sea again.
Winds nestled in their great white wings,
And rainbows arched each prow,
With streaming banners on they sped ; —
Why clouds his furrowed brow ?

The old man sits and ponders
When night winds vex the sea,
And booming billows pain his ear
With awful prophecy.
Alas ! his treasures bring no joy,
His sleep is not repose —
Like the deep rush of the river
His restless being flows.

His stately ships return no more ;
He bends beneath his care,
But still looks out upon the deep
To see if they are there ;
His brain grows faint with thinking,
For thoughts like spectres rise,

Till the soothing hand of slumber
  Softly shuts his aching eyes.

He sports *now* by the streamlet,
  In the meadows green and wide,
He sees his ships of lilies
  On the sunny ripples glide ;
The soft breeze wantons with his hair,
  His heart leaps blithe and free —
But hush ! no breath — a shoreless main
  Bears on life's argosy.

1852.

IMPROMPTU FAREWELL TO ESTES PARK.

THROUGH the sweet air these glorious mountains rise —
Their sun-bright summits in the silent skies.
O Vale of Peace! in their strong arms caressed,
With our farewells are memories doubly blest.
As onward in Time's devious path we go,
In pictured thought these royal scenes shall glow.
Oh, may our lives thus rise more bright and grand,
Till we upon the heavenly mountains stand.

BY FAITH.

BY FAITH.

THE NEW BIRTH.

ES, all is plain ! I see,
I live, I am made free !
O Love, my new-found guest !
Sweet peace, and sweetest rest !
What shall I do, what say,
In this rare morn which is true life's first day ?
All round are odors blown,
And with soft undertone
Faint music pants in all the glowing air.
The waters call in many a flower-fringed stream ;
The earth is very fair,
And through the depths of tender sky
Floats many a cloud-bright argosy ;
But I have tasted something more divine.
I see a glory brighter than the May ;
I hear what seraphs to each other say ;

A heavenly heart is throbbing against mine.
These earthly blossoms cannot make my crown,
Celestial strains this earthly music drown,
I look, as through an open door,
On landscapes that shall fade no more.

O Saviour, Jesus, it is all of Thee —
This sacred sense of what I 'm made to be,
Thy perfect self and my infirmity ; —
All, all of Thee — the veil removed,
The joy that springs in being loved,
The faith that asks no higher place
Than sights of Thy forgiving face.

Nearer and nearer, Lord, and nearer still,
Thy work begun, fulfill,
Shape all my life according to Thy will.
Thou knowest how I aspire ;
Accept my strong desire,
Hope, heart, and mind — my spirit's deepest deep —
Take all, to feed and keep,
Till my whole soul to Love's full flower is blown,
And Love's full flower to perfect fruit is grown.

"ABIDE WITH US: FOR IT IS TOWARD EVENING."

THE tender light is fading where
  We pause and linger still,
And, through the dim and saddened air,
  We feel the evening chill.

Long hast Thou journeyed with us, Lord,
  Ere we Thy face did know ;
Oh, still Thy fellowship afford,
  While dark the shadows grow.

For passed is many a beauteous field,
  Beside our morning road ;
And many a fount to us is sealed,
  That once so freshly flowed.

The splendor of the noontide lies
  On other paths than ours ;
The dews that lave yon fragrant skies
  Will not revive our flowers.

It is not now as in the glow
  Of life's impassioned heat,

When to the heart there seemed to flow
  All that of earth was sweet.

Something has faded — something died,
  Without us and within ;
We, more than ever, need a guide,
  Blinded and weak with sin.

The weight is heavy that we bear,
  Our strength more feeble grows ;
Weary with toil, and pain, and care,
  We long for sweet repose.

Stay with us, gracious Saviour, stay,
  While friends and hopes depart ;
Fainting, on Thee we wish to lay
  The burden of our heart.

Abide with us, dear Lord, remain,
  Our Life, our Truth, our Way,
So shall our loss be turned to gain —
  Night dawn to endless day.

1864.

"THY COMFORTS DELIGHT MY SOUL."

I KNOW the fair, green earth is Thine,
And Thine, O Lord, the starry heaven ;
From Thee the blessed light doth shine,
By Thee the soft, sweet air is given ;
And dear are all the common things
That tell of love from day to day —
The bud that blooms, the bird that sings,
And tender faces round my way.

'T is not that any gift from Thee
Is less than perfect, that I prize
The comforts of Thy grace to me
Above the sights of earth and skies.
Thyself Supreme, Eternal Good,
Art more than all Thy works disclose.
O Lamb of God! Thy sacred blood
To me Love's deepest secret shows.

From mortal ills I am not free,
Nor have I walked an easy road ;
Yet every step was best for me,
Since by the Man of Sorrows trode.

Through all my dark has shone Thy face,
  Thy peace has flowed beneath my pain,
Stumbling, I fell in Thy embrace,
  My loss by Thee was turned to gain.

And I might tell of hours apart,
  In lonely path and secret place,
When burned and glowed within my heart
  The wondrous meanings of Thy grace.
Enough that Thou did'st there abide,
  And break the bread, and call me friend;—
Thy comforts, O Thou Crucified!
  Refresh me to my journey's end.

No wonder that my weary feet
  Grow strong in sight of Calvary;
That all Thy gifts are passing sweet,
  Embalmed in love so great and free.
Thy perfect beauty dawns more dear,
  As nearer to Thy cross I come;
In Thee my life is only clear,
  Thy heart, O Christ, is Heaven and Home.

SUNDAY EVENING.

The twilight of the evening lies
On quiet homes and tender skies.
The sacred silence seems to bring
A blessing on its brooding wing,
And all the hallowed Sabbath air
Is like the calm of silent prayer.

O precious calm! O healing rest!
That broods so warmly in my breast:
It seems that on my life doth lie
The peace that soothes the upper sky, —
A large contentment, in whose grace
Joy wells like light in liberal space, —
A tranquil trust, a hope whose eye
Is full of immortality,
And love whose sweetness freshens through
My being like celestial dew.

Thanks! Father, that thy Church once more
On life's vain strife has shut the door,
And to a holy feast doth win
Her waiting, wandering children in.

Thanks! for thy grace has been to-day
More than we dared to hope or pray;
Thy cloud of mercy hung above
Has broken with the weight of love!

EMMANUEL.

God with us!
Lo, the mystery is unraveled!
O earth and ages which in pain have travailed
With grievous lamentation, cease to mourn.
The garments of your praise put on,
O Zion! raise your drooping head!
Arise and shine, O prostrate one!
On thee the balms of Paradise are shed.
He comes! Deliverer! King!
The nations' expectation and desire;
Your crowns of glory fling,
In rapturous adoration, Heavenly choir!
Fly, blessed news, on Love's ecstatic wing!
Sad world, rejoice, your dreadful discord cease,
Good will on earth has come, and holy Peace!

God with us!
Light fills gloomy habitations,
Hope shines on faces furrowed deep with tears,
From desert lands triumphant gratulations
Resound adown the glad applauding years.

No more need Sorrow moan,
With blank, despairing eyes,
Or Reason grope alone
'Neath stern and pitiless skies;
Or Guilt with smoking altars strive to win
From outraged Justice, pardon for its sin.
O poor and frail humanity,
The largess of your ransom see!
Primeval Eden is restored,
God is with us, the Lord!

God with us!
It is for you, sick heart,
Pierced with contrition's dart;
And you who in your household blight,
By empty cradles and the vacant chair,
Long for the old delight
Of joyous hearths and faces sweet and fair;
For you who see your morning visions die
Before the dew has vanished from your prime;
And you who, with strong supplications, cry
For thrones and crowns of the eternal clime,
God is with you!

God with us!
Hear it, burdened ones and weary,
Who toil beneath the lash, without a home;
And you who pine in chambers chill and dreary,
Wond'ring when sweet release and rest will come;

And you who seek, with vain caresses,
  To win a smile from pallid lips of clay
Yet thrilling at the touch of beauteous tresses,
  But seeing all your comforts far away.
    Oh, hear it, all who think your care
    Is more than you can bear,
    Halting, and stumbling on with bruised feet;
    Accept the message sweet,
          God is with you!

          God with us!
Yea, with *you*, who, drowsed in sin,
Feel not the fatal leprosy within,
  Thankless and prayerless in your proud estate;
    With you who crouch away in shame
  From homes in which you were the light of late;
    With you who dare proclaim
    Contempt of the Beloved Name;
    On you, with pitying grace,
    He turns the awful sorrow of his face,
And still through cold and darkness stands,
Knocking at flinty hearts with bleeding hands;
    Oh, give Him place!
          God is with you!

ECCLESIA.

I SAW the shining of uncounted faces,
Sweet placid brows and eyes of silent prayer,
The holy ones whose lives make sacred places,
And sow with beauty regions that were bare:

Great seers and prophets of the elder ages,
Singers that melt us into joyous tears,
Strong souls that blazon on immortal pages
The mystic legends of Love's fruitful years ;

Captains and conquerors in the unseen sieges
When fortressed wrong and secret sin were slain,
Fair white-robed spirits, valiant loving lieges
Of Him through whom they died and rose again.

All round went patient feet on errands holy,
And gracious hands were doing noble things ;
None boasted there — the lofty and the lowly
In that blest company were priests and kings.

Some walked amid the blossoms of their beauty
Joy crowned and radiant with their quenchless dream,

And some, forgetting self in tasks of duty,
Saw not the nimbus o'er their foreheads beam.

Some stood amid war's blinding smoke and thunder,
With Freedom's promise flashing in their eyes,
And some, on lone and flinty heights, bent under
The heavy cross of daily sacrifice.

And some in patience toiled, with mighty yearning,
For truths of which men dream, but do not see,
And with exultant hope beheld the burning
Of error's chaff and regal effigy.

And some, in sacred chambers hushed and shaded,
Waited the angel of a blest release ;
And some, who through the turbid depths had waded,
At last basked on the sun-crowned hills of peace.

Round smiling hearths where children sport and nestle,
In minsters old, and closets sweet with prayer,
In clam'rous marts where giant forces wrestle,
In lonely ranche and attics bleak and bare,

Where'er souls catch the light and voice supernal,
And in the Spirit do the Master's will,
There are "The Called" — beloved of the Eternal —
Whose scattered ranks the Heavenly courts shall fill.

www.ingramcontent.com/pod-product-compliance
Lightning Source LLC
LaVergne TN
LVHW021412110826
845150LV00007B/1887

* 9 7 8 1 4 2 5 5 1 1 1 8 0 *